LAST SUMMER

A Little Book for Dads

RAQUEL JARAMILLO

Andrews McMeel
Publishing

Kansas City

Last summer I was still afraid of the ocean.

The waves seemed so big.
And I felt so little.

I would stand at the edge of the water
where the waves could not reach me.

I would make footprints in the sand.

I would crush the tiny water bubbles with my toes.

I would shout at the waves.

But I would not go in.

No way would I go in.

One day, as the sun was going down, my daddy
taught me how not to be afraid.

He told me to look at the whole ocean—not just the waves.

Waves come and go, he explained. They crash and make a lot of noise.

But they're only a small part of the ocean.

You have to look past the waves, he said.

He even got his feet wet to show me there
was nothing to be afraid of.

And then he walked me to the water.

First I got my feet wet.

And then I got my hands wet.

It took some getting used to.

But soon I realized I was not afraid.
I was just wet.

I was so happy I started laughing at the waves.
"Ha-ha! I'm not afraid of you anymore!"

And I danced a victory dance.

Last summer, my daddy taught me something I will never forget.

If you look past the waves,
you will always see the ocean.

For Lela, across the sea

04 05 06 07 08 KFO 10 9 8 7 6 5 4 3 2 1

ISBN: 0-7407-4186-1

ATTENTION: SCHOOLS AND BUSINESSES

Andrews McMeel books are available at quantity discounts with bulk purchase for educational, business, or sales promotional use. For information, please write to: Special Sales Department, Andrews McMeel Publishing, 4520 Main Street, Kansas City, Missouri 64111.